# THE POWER OF PERSPECTIVE

*Gaining Clarity Purpose & Truth
Through Affirmation*

## TR ARMSTRONG

*When you wake up every day, you have two choices. You can either be positive or negative; an optimist or a pessimist. I choose to be an optimist. It's all a matter of perspective.*

—HARVEY MACKAY

*With the sincerest of hearts, I want to say a big THANK YOU to my friends, family and all those who have supported me in my journey. I love you all. I am also grateful and thankful for all experiences, good and bad. For without which I would not have been put on the path to clarity, purpose, truth and eventually redemption.*

\- TR Armstrong

# PREFACE

Trying to gain some perspective, I began to reflect on a lot of things. We tend to do that when things aren't going right. Or better yet, the way we think they should go. Focusing on negatives and asking ourselves, what went wrong. Full of self-pity. Crawling deeper and deeper into our pain. It's much easier to do that, than to accept responsibility and take control. But I knew that was what I had to do. Take control. Things would not improve until I did.

I started reflecting on the good things. The positive choices I'd made. Zooming in and magnifying them to give me a point of reference. Using them to lay the foundation I needed to attain the growth, success and perspective I so desperately wanted.

Some define perspective as simply a point of view, or way of thinking. I believe it is much more than that. I like to think of perspective as a sense of gaining, learning and realizing. So that you can take what you've learned and grow from the inside out.

Perspective allows you to make choices and decisions that will help, not hinder, your progress. I say this because until I changed how I viewed my life, relationships, choices and my perceived helplessness in my own destiny- nothing I attempted to do worked out.

By seeing my life as a series of failures; a string of missed and wasted opportunities, I was conceding defeat before I even started. Nothing good can come about with a thought process that is habitually and consistently negative.

The good news is that regardless of how you view the world, you can change that view at any time. You simply make a choice and hold yourself accountable to that choice. That power belongs to you and only you.

When I allowed myself to realize that it didn't matter where I was or what I did up until that point, my future was my own, I was then able to focus on the possibilities. Focus on who I was, and where I wanted to be. I understood that if I approached things with the proper perspective and let that be my compass, I would eventually get there.

Making positive life choices needs to be a habit. Second nature so you don't have to think about it or ask yourself if you're doing the right thing. You will already know. Instinct and intuition will guide you. Allow those realizations to shape your perception. Once you've done that, things will begin to come together.

You will have the ability to put things in their proper place. Recognize and encourage what adds value to your life, as well as understanding and erasing that which doesn't. This leaves you free to look past who you are now and see who you have the power and ability to become.

# INTRODUCTION

These affirmations are universal. Aimed at the heart, the soul, of the broken and enlightened alike. They are not so much rules, but guidelines and principles for living a more peaceful existence. By heightening your awareness of the role our thoughts, actions and choices play in shaping one's perspective, you will be able to maintain clarity when you need it most.

Many never realize that they have lost perspective until a critical point is reached in their lives where that very perspective is necessary to rise above whatever adversity is interrupting their transition and transcendence to a better and more meaningful existence.

Now these aren't the typical or traditional uplifting phrases dedicated to helping you have a positive day. No, these are deeper and longer. Their purpose aimed at helping you have a positive life. Not just to motivate or inspire you, but to push you beyond the scope of comprehension and rationality.

I don't just want to tell you but show you the possibilities that exist when you wipe your mental state clean of all the clutter that exists solely to distract you from your destiny. To help you break through the barriers of resistance that exist between you and purpose so that you can, not only realize but pursue, attain total clarity. Then you will begin to live the most productive life possible.

When you rid yourself of the mental and emotional distractions of this world, you are free to evolve your thought process from one of needs and wants, to one of will and purpose. No longer driven by pettiness and ego, but instead destiny and truth. That moment you realize that everything you thought you wanted, thought you knew, was nothing but an unrealistic distraction from true joy and fulfilment. In doing so denying yourself the clarity and peace of mind that comes with true perspective.

I admit, I myself was arrogant and indignant. Always justifying my actions (and reactions) so that I was never wrong. I was driven by self-importance. And thanks to my ego I was also lonely, broken, angry and alone. Living without substance or purpose. Watching impatiently as the world continued to move on without me. Leaving me envious of all that I wanted, but which continued to elude me. At least until I began to hold myself accountable. Until I took full responsibility and regained the perspective I was choosing to ignore.

Every one of these passages was born out of a moment, experience, interaction or event that affected me in the deepest parts of my soul. Sometimes it was joy. Others it was pain. From infidelity and addiction, to depression and eventually accountability. Each experience led me to a place of reflection and inevitable acceptance. It didn't happen overnight. The journey to reach the point of understanding that I now possess, took longer than I would have liked. But that impatience was an indication that I still wasn't ready. I needed to trust the process, go through the motions. I couldn't skip any steps if I truly wanted to reach a place of peace and fluidity that would make me pause. Make me take a step back before reacting to situations in a manner I knew would be regretted sometime later.

This book is my way of sharing what helped me find truth and purpose within myself. There was a point in time when I thought I would hurt forever. Believing that my destiny was to be forever trapped in my tortured mind. Consumed with negative thoughts and reliving my missteps eternally. Every disappointment, bad decision, broken heart and opportunity lost (or squandered) replaying endlessly. But things did get better. I crawled out of the wreckage of my past purposeful and enlightened. I was now hungry for life and living. I hope that with this book, by taking this journey with me, you will too.

# ONE

*'I wanted you to see what real courage is, instead of getting
the idea that courage is a man with a gun in his hand. It's
when you know you're licked before you begin, but you begin
anyway and see it through no matter what.'*

—*Atticus Finch (To Kill A Mockingbird)*

They say courage is venturing into the unknown. Moving forward when the outcome is uncertain. This much is true. However, are you brave enough to move forward when you know the outcome and that it will be painful? To know that your heart will be broken in unspeakable ways, and no matter what you do the ending will remain the same? Not when, just that it will.

Would you still make the journey? One vital to your acknowledgement of self. Instrumental in the gaining of truth, enlightenment and understanding. Would you be brave enough to endure to reach the other side of your destiny?

Allow your heart to be touched by bonds that transcend love? Silent and unspeakable chains on your heart. Every laugh, every smile etched. And every tear embedded in your soul. Would you have the courage to allow yourself to experience all that you have to and gain the perspective you need to impact the world.

# TWO

*'We don't develop courage by being happy every day. We develop it by surviving difficult times and challenging adversity.*

—*Barbara De Angelis*

Never forget how strong you are. Despite where you are mentally or emotionally, you have the strength to make it to the other side of pain. Everything you want, everything you need to survive is within you.

Use adversity to your advantage. Stare it in the face and turn it on its head. Take all the pain, fear and anxiety that has crippled you; use that energy as the fuel you need to fight back. Compel and propel yourself beyond all the things that have held you back. Kept you from life and from living.

Deny negativity entry into your mind, your heart- your soul. Commit to moving on and moving forward. Be a force so strong that it scares you and everyone around you. Be fearless in your quest for success. Reclaim you power. Take it and run so far and so fast that nothing can stop you.

Keep going until you reach the threshold of reason and insanity, purpose and truth. Where your destiny awaits.

# THREE

*Your purpose in life is to find your purpose and give your whole heart and soul to it.*

—*Buddha*

You are the architect of your future and the designer of your destiny. The life that you are living right here, right now was created specifically for you. By you. It's not an imitation or duplication of anyone else's purpose.

While there are many who feel that you can somehow manipulate destiny, you can't just place your feet on the prints left in the sand by another and expect to reach the same destination. For it isn't just the journey, but the sincerity of that journey that is the key to unlocking your purpose.

# FOUR

*'Don't talk, act. Don't say, show. Don't promise, prove.'*

*—Anonymous*

Listen to what others say, but more importantly watch what they do. Take note of contradictions and inconsistencies. Hold them accountable to their words, and responsible for their actions. It is okay to show and give respect solely at one's word but be sure to let them know that if they said it you heard it- and you will hold them to it. Give the benefit of the doubt with the highest esteem and expectation. Judge them on their commitment to their word, and the capability of upholding it.

# FIVE

*'But merely being tradition does not make something worthy.*
*We can't assume that because something is old it is right.'*

—*Brandon Sanderson*

If you want to live a deeper, more meaningful and purposeful life you must be willing to sacrifice and fight. Do away with all that you think you know and resist the temptations of ego.

Break the rules of rationality so that you are free to accept new possibilities. Release your mind from the chains of tradition and past choices. Surrender your soul to the unknown. Only with an open heart and untethered conscience will you be able to tap into that part of your unbiased soul that transcends judgement, morality and desire. Thereby giving you the freedom to fulfil your true destiny.

# SIX

*'GOD never gave a lion teeth for decoration.'*

—*Matshona Dhliwayo*

We have all been given gifts that set us apart. A talent unlike any other that only we can use to its fullest potential. They individualize and separate us from the pack. Whether you were born to be a doctor, painter, attorney or chef. A writer, singer, mother or teacher. Tap into the power you've been given. Harness and cultivate it. Nurture and share it.

In a world of gifts, grab them while you can. Do this because you have a responsibility, not just to yourself, but the world to take the gifts you've been given and use them.

# SEVEN

*'If you dare nothing, then when the day is over, nothing is all
you will have gained.'*

—*Neil Gaiman (The Graveyard Book)*

Don't settle for being comfortable. Sliding through life unnoticed and under the radar. Doing just enough to get by. PLAY BIG! Bold and loud; take risks. Challenge yourself by pushing past the scope of rational thinking and comprehension. Take yourself to imaginable heights and free fall into destiny.

Let fate take your hand and guide you into a predestined journey to the other side of thinking. Mental and emotional bliss unencumbered by the distractions of normality.

# EIGHT

*'Stop validating your victim mentality. Shake off your self-defeating drama and embrace your innate ability to recover and achieve.'*

—*Dr. Steve Maraboli*

TODAY I will stop playing the victim.
Self-importance is my worst enemy.
As long as I continue to be a victim, I will never progress.
This stops today!

From today forward I understand that I no longer make mistakes,
I make choices.
Today I take responsibility for all I am and all that I will be.

Today I am full of energy and life. I can do anything. Today I am humble, yet strong.
I accept all criticism with optimism.

# NINE

*'A teachable spirit is being willing to be a student in any area you lack, to seek out knowledge and truth, in order to grow in humility, wisdom and excellence.'*

*—Unknown*

Life is full of teachable moments. Some teach us about others, and some teach us about ourselves. In these moments we not only learn what we are made of, but we learn what others are capable of.

There is no belief more dangerous than the assumption that one knows everything. There is always something left to learn.

Seek knowledge at every turn from all areas of life. A truly wise person, when they are being challenged internally, will recognize the opportunity presented to take something away. Even if it is learning something unflattering about themselves.

# TEN

*'You gotta be original, because if you're like someone else,
what do they need you for?'*

—*Bernadette Peters*

There comes a time when you must grow up. Stop searching for what you want and start manifesting what you need. Create and use your own experiences as the example. Instead of looking to be impressed, look to be inspired. And in turn be an inspiration. You can't take someone else's passion and make it your own. You cannot imitate, duplicate or recreate likeability and truth. Know who you are and what your purpose is.

# ELEVEN

*'Have a vision. It is the ability to see the invisible. If you can see the invisible, you can achieve the impossible.'*

—*Shiv Khera*

Don't just think about your goals, but how you're going to push yourself after you've attained them. Ask yourself, 'How can I, will I give back to those on the same path?' Encourage and support others. Be an example of how the impossible can indeed be achieved. Move full steam ahead with zero doubt about the greatness that the present and future hold. The improbable becomes the possible and the world's blessings become yours.

# TWELVE

*'I embraced everything that I thought would hold me back
from pursuing my dreams and used my insecurities to give me
the courage to inspire and advocate for others...'*

—La'Porsha Renae

The unwillingness to acknowledge another's accomplishments betrays an arrogance and ego so strong that it renders some helpless in the face of grace and humility. Missing the opportunity to grow as needed to achieve one's own hopes and dreams. Instead, languishing in mediocrity and constantly banging their head against the wall of progression. Unable to understand why things aren't moving forward despite their best efforts. The inability to grasp the significance and importance of championing others, will undoubtedly lead to a failure to manifest a champion of your own. Know better and be better than that.

# THIRTEEN

*'I never get sullen, sad or envious, because those emotions will get me nowhere.'*

—Aditya Roy Kapur

The most covetous and envious people are sometimes the ones closest to you. They can be friends, family, co-workers or acquaintances. It's important to recognize these people so you can distance yourself if necessary.

Appreciate, congratulate, compliment and reciprocate. Vital elements to relationship success that many find hard to do. Instead they use their wins as an opportunity to knock you down and point ow what they would've done that was better or different. What you should've done but didn't. All to make you feel inadequate. This is a passive aggressive behavior that is insidious and toxic. The great think about perspective is that it not only helps us recognize our own negative behaviors, but the negativity in those around us as well.

# FOURTEEN

*'Knowing why you are is your purpose.*
*Knowing who you are is your style.*
*Knowing what you are is your character.'*

—Debasish Mridha

Be comfortable and fearless in the face of others' interpretation of you. Know who you are. Your character, your heart and your intent. While one should not allow themselves to be burdened by the responsibilities of others, be humble. Humble enough to know and understand that your opinions and beliefs are your own as well, and not the responsibility of others to agree with, support or take on. There is strength in humility. You must be prepared to stand alone so that you can stand out.

# FIFTEEN

*'Look beneath the surface; let not the several quality of a thing
nor its worth escape the.'*

*—Ashley Lorenzana*

We use our experiences and our choices to create a barrier between our surface
and our soul. Afraid to flay the skin of the past and expose an unknown future. If you
are persistent and focused; determined and faithful you will uncover and discover
that what lies beneath is worth all the time and energy put forth in the journey to
something deeper, meaningful and lasting.

# SIXTEEN

*'The truth is, unless you let go, unless you forgive yourself,
unless you forgive the situation, unless you realize that the
situation is over, you cannot move forward.'*

—*Steve Maraboli*

Do you use your past like a ruler to measure all current and future relationships? Are you constantly weighing your purpose on the scale of past choices? Already tilting from decisions no longer in your control. Making it possible to ever be level. Free yourself from the distractions of guilt and you will soon find the scales of universal justice tilting in your favor.

# SEVENTEEN

*'All great changes are preceded by chaos.'*

—*Deepak Chopra*

Every person on this planet has a purpose. Contrary to popular belief, that purpose isn't always positive. Some exist to upset the natural order. To shake things up; wreak havoc and cause chaos. This is an important and necessary purpose because it acts as a catalyst. To jumpstart those, yourself included, who have resigned themselves to a complacent and rational existence knowing you were meant for so much more.

# EIGHTEEN

*'The universe has shaken you to awaken you.'*

*—Mastin Kipp*

I consider a petty tyrant to be a gift. Placed in your life purposefully to force you out of that comfortable and stable feeling that living a predictable and ordinary life provides. Settling for the familiar and accepting the known as truth when your fate, your destiny has something much greater waiting for you.

The universe has gifts for you that transcend the conceivable, the ordinary and the rational. Trouble placed in our path to shake the very foundation of all you've subscribed to until that moment you realize that there are no promises. No guarantees. No right or wrong. That different isn't bad, it's just different. So, you can rid yourself of all that holds you back physically and metaphorically speaking. Forge ahead without fear or reservation. Grow, develop and evolve into the best version of yourself capable. Continue with the process over and over until you have shed every layer of acceptance, of excuses and have reached the highest level of clarity.

# NINETEEN

*'When I pass, speak freely of my shortcomings and my flaws.*
*Learn from them, for I'll have no ego to injure.'*

*—Aaron McGruder*

That we are human should forever make us humble. It is a constant reminder that we are a flawed species. Our existence is doubt filled and ego driven. Traits that left unchecked and unbalanced will do no less than lead us down a path of self-destruction.

The good news is that there is truth on the other side. Our humanity is also coupled with free will and choice, and with that the ability to move in ways and directions that are controlled by wisdom and perspective. Making us capable of not only pursuing, but achieving excellence.

# TWENTY

*'Our intention creates our reality.'*

—*Wayne Dyer*

Be persistent, purposeful and pure in your intention. Be 100% aware and accountable to your choices. Pursue the highest state of clarity and perspective possible. Where excellence and divinity meet and are intertwined. Where one can't exist without the other and you know that you have fulfilled a necessary part of the journey to be your best self.

# TWENTY-ONE

*'If you are never scared, embarrassed or hurt, it means you never take chances.'*

—*Julia Soul*

Avoid living a shallow life. Always treading water just to stay afloat. Never really going for it. Never taking the plunge. You must be willing to dive into the deep end of thinking and explore what else is out there, instead of being afraid of the abyss. If you shed that fear, you will find your place within the bigger, larger universe.

# TWENTY-TWO

*'Perspective is everything when you are experiencing the challenges of life.'*

—*Joni Eareckson Tada*

A life and a path to greatness is within your grasp if you are willing to recognize and accept the inherent fallacies that exist within. Acknowledge and succumb to a higher source of power, learning and truth. Seek and choose perspective. Allow it to widen your perceptions of the world. Not just around you, but beyond you as well.

# TWENTY-THREE

*'Change is the law of life. And those who look only to the past or present are certain to miss the future.'*

—*John F. Kennedy*

Live to make memories, moments and milestones. Don't settle for a life riddled with wasted time, missed opportunities or painful regrets. Buy a one-way ticket to destiny and don't look back. Nor should you hold back or turn back on your journey. Leave the choices you've made behind you so that you can savor every joyous moment ahead.

# TWENTY-FOUR

*'I think a lot of people have lost respect for the individual, you know, the individual, the person who doesn't conform.'*

—*Erykah Badu*

Do not get caught up in the hype of what everyone else is doing. Resist the temptation to go with the flow. Getting swept away and lost in a sea of conformity. You have your own destiny to fulfill and the journey to get there only you can dictate. Through behaviors and actions that will take you on a winding road of good and bad. Ups, downs; wins and losses. You will eventually and inevitably arrive at a point of clarity, enlightenment, personal choice and truth.

# TWENTY-FIVE

*'Not caring more about what other people think than what you think. That's freedom.'*

—Demi Moore

What others do, say or believe about you is not your concern. It is not your will to be dominated or defeated, but instead to conquer and triumph. To silence all the naysayers and quell the negativity that exists to create barriers of distraction between you and destiny. To quiet those wanting to disrupt the progress you've achieved on the road to independence, growth and purpose.

# TWENTY-SIX

*'People grow through experience if they meet life honestly and courageously. This is how character is built.'*

—*Eleanor Roosevelt*

You will know you have reached an uninhibited, unbothered and unbiased level of growth when the things that bothered you yesterday, no longer bother you today. Situations and choices that have weighed heavy on your mind are no longer a part of your thought process. No longer will you be overwhelmed with internal chaos, but instead you will simply smile and carry on living. Oblivious to the existing distractions because they will no longer have access to your progress.

# TWENTY-SEVEN

*'I don't want to follow in anyone's footsteps. I want to follow my own path and do something unique.'*

—*Kris Wu*

Do not follow in the footsteps of another's journey. Refuse to let your life be dictated, defined or directed by someone else's perception or perspective. Be the driver of your own destiny. Free from comfort and contentment. Leave the impression on this world that your purpose wills you to.

# TWENTY-EIGHT

*'Yes, I'm seeking for someone to help me. So that someday, I
will be the someone to help some other one.'*

—*Vignesh Karthi*

The path to learning, believing and accepting who you are and what your purpose is, doesn't have to be travelled alone. As we grow, it is normal to experience crises of identity and choice. Not only questioning who we are and where we're going, but where we fit in the lives of those closest to us. To be a better communicator, partner, lover or friend, include them on your journey to self-discovery. This is important because who you become will be futile if those you love remain un-enlightened, and have themselves remained unchanged.

# TWENTY-NINE

*'It is in your moments of decision that your destiny is shaped.'*

*—Tony Robbins*

Are you at a crossroads? Are you standing at the junction of living, where duty and choice intersect? When intention manifests deep within forcing duty and choice to go their separate ways. No longer having the same interests in kind.

Duty leads to fate; that predictable destination mapped by tradition and rationality. Whereas choice leads to destiny. And with it a journey wrought with excitement, unpredictability and joy.

# THIRTY

*'Remember, the world will judge you based on how you judge yourself.'*

—*Vincent Mueller*

We all have moments of anxiety, apprehension and uncertainty. But as difficult as it may seem, you must push yourself past the point of self-doubt and believe. Trust yourself. Trust your instincts. Be confident enough to break free of arrogance, and humble enough to leave ego behind. Follow your heart and what it tells you. Tap into your inner strength and let your soul guide you.

# THIRTY-ONE

*'The only person you are destined to become, is the person you decide to be.'*

—*Ralph Waldo Emerson*

What would you do if you knew that your heart, your soul was at stake; at risk of extinction? What would you be willing to sacrifice in order to get back that feeling you once had when you dared to dream? When you dared to believe that anything was possible and had the audacity to follow your heart. Pursued that which gave you the greatest pleasure.

Would you stare fear in the face with unbridled confidence? Battle adversity head to head? Abandon hope and instead place your unconditional faith in destiny? To let your hopes be resurrected and bring you back from the brink of emotional extinction, hungry for life?

# THIRTY-TWO

*'Whatever we are waiting for – peace of mind, contentment, grace, the inner awareness of simple abundance – it will surely come to us, but only when we are ready to receive it with an open and grateful heart.'*

—*Sarah Ban Breathnach*

Live a grateful life steeped in humility. Let it bring you closer to grace. Allow your humanity to be broken down to the core and exposed in its rawest form. Exposing a soul shrouded in serenity. When you are in a divine and peaceful state of being, purpose escapes you not and destiny is within reach.

# THIRTY-THREE

*'Ignore self-doubt and inner conflict. Dwell on positive thoughts.'*

*—Lailah Gifty Akita*

As a human being, it is not only inherent, but inevitable to have doubts and fears. Inner struggles and external troubles. Emotions and actions detrimental to all you have accomplished will at times creep into your safety zone of thinking and shake you up a bit. But it is important that you recognize when your perspective is in danger and not allow seeds to be planted, nor poisonous roots to grow that will choke the life out of your progress.

# THIRTY-FOUR

*'What you see depends not only on what you look AT, but also,*
*on where you look FROM.'*

—*James Deacon*

The power that perspective holds is that it gives you the ability to look beyond hopes and expectations and reject all excuses. This makes way for you to take responsibility for your choices and hold yourself accountable to the consequences of those choices.

Perspective doesn't condone, it challenges. It pushes you to the very edge of thinking, leaving you free to jump headfirst into the deep end of life; of living. It frees you from all the distractions that have held you captive and prevented you from living your best life. So, consumed with mental and emotional chaos that you lose yourself. Losing the part of you that is passionate and driven.

Don't watch your dreams disappear into the darkness. Drowning in a sea of doubt. Perspective is the life raft that keeps you from accepting and settling for a life you no longer recognize as your own.

# THIRTY-FIVE

*'The purpose of life is not to be happy. It is to be useful, to be honorable, to be compassionate, to have it make some difference that you have lived and lived well.'*

—*Ralph Waldo Emerson*

Life is not fair, easy or deserving. But you can level the playing field by choosing to live with purpose. The pursuit of excellence is what separates those distracted by what they think they deserve and those who pursue that which they know they are destined.

# THIRTY-SIX

*'Self-care is how you take your power back.'*

—*Lalah Delia*

We all need to take a step back at times to regroup and recharge. Confronted daily with situations and choices that can be overwhelming, I wake each morning and simply breathe. Relax my mind and clear all the clutter so that I can start my day with the mental strength and capacity to make positive and perspective filled choices. It's this strength that gives me the power to take charge of the day and move forward without reservations or hesitation.

# THIRTY-SEVEN

*'Passion is energy. Feel the power that comes from focusing on what excites you.'*

—*Oprah Winfrey*

Be filled with an insatiable hunger and an unquenchable thirst. Let every goal reached and every accomplishment achieved fuel the fire within you. Refuse to let your passions fall to the wayside and die a slow death. Instead, fans the flames of destiny.

# THIRTY-EIGHT

*'There is one word which may serve as a rule of practice for all one's life – reciprocity.'*

—*Confucius*

Don't simply take but give something positive back to everyone in your life. Too few appreciate the need and value of reciprocity. Use your relationships to make yourself a better person while enriching someone else as well. Let your interactions with others push and challenge you so that you can be better to them; for them. Use that knowledge to improve all aspects of your life.

# THIRTY-NINE

*'Starve your distractions. Feed your focus.'*

—*Charmaine Hayden*

When you rid yourself of distraction, the perspective gained will afford you the wisdom and clarity to know what disruptions are in your path. Lying in wait, attempting to derail you. Shed arrogance and ego so that your heart and mind are open to receive life's blessings.

# FORTY

*'Life is too short to spend on warring. Fight only the most, most, most important ones, let the rest go.'*

—C. JoyBell C.

No matter where you are on the path to enlightenment, never underestimate or take for granted that there will always be people and situations placed in your path to test you. Test your patience, test your faith and most importantly test your grace.

Picking your battles is of the utmost importance. Perspective affords you the wisdom to know that it is little more than a distraction. One whose sole purpose is to throw you into mental and emotional disarray. Attempting to halt your journey to an ultimately healthier and more meaningful mental state of being.

# FORTY-ONE

*'You could say that arrogance is false confidence and that the person displaying it is overcompensating for their inner inadequacies'*

*—Stewart Stafford*

The line between arrogance and confidence can be blurry if you lack perspective. Arrogance is inherently selfish. Driven by ego and self-importance. But confidence shows strength, courage and faith. Not just in yourself, but in others as well.

Where arrogance sees competition, confidence sees partnership and collaboration. The intrinsic value of being another's advocate is not lost. A confident person is humble enough to know that by helping others, you also help yourself.

# FORTY-TWO

*'There is a life-force within your soul, seek that life.'*

*—Rumi*

What you want is within reach, but what you need is within you. You already possess the tools needed to regain your strength, reclaim your power and realize your truth. Rid yourself of self-doubt by banishing negative thoughts and actions that have interrupted your ascension to a purposeful life. Let passion be the driving force that propels you past fear and closer to fulfillment.

# FORTY-THREE

*'The only courage that matters is the kind that gets you from one moment to the next.'*

—*Richard Bachman*

Take each day as it comes and make it a priority. Not a week, month or year. Just one day. Live in the moment and treat each day with the perspective it deserves, and in the capacity needed so that you can move forward positively.

If you wake up every day knowing, owning and accepting that your life is in your hands, and hold yourself accountable to that fact, you will be well on your way to realizing your potential.

# FORTY-FOUR

*'I seek strength, not to be greater than another, but to fight my greatest enemy, the doubts within myself.'*

—*P.C. Cast*

There will always be outside forces in your path designed to distract you from your purpose, but the one you must fight the hardest is the force inside of you. Be strong and focused on the journey to self-discovery. Be prepared to go toe to toe with fear, pound for pound with doubt and round after round with ego until you emerge victorious.

# FORTY-FIVE

*'Your past is not your destiny. You can change your future at any moment.'*

—*Anthon St. Maarten*

Stop using the past to avoid taking responsibility in the present. Blaming others and focusing on what they may have done to impede your growth and prevent your success. Instead of focusing on the negative, reflect on the positive. Think about how the positive choices you've made have affected your life for the better and repeat them. Lay the foundation you need to reach the level of growth required to achieve excellence.

When you stop allowing the past to weigh you down, you will be free. No longer helpless, but capable. No longer pessimistic, but hopeful.

# FORTY-SIX

*'If you get your ego in the way, you will only look to other
people and circumstances to blame.'*

—Jocko Willink

Do you have what it takes to resist the temptations of ego? Do you possess the courage necessary to free yourself from a self-important way of thinking, living and being? Raise your level of consciousness and free your mind. Accept freedom and free will as a way of life.

# FORTY-SEVEN

*'Alone we can do so little; together we can do so much.'*

—*Helen Keller*

Many mistakenly believe that to work on yourself it needs to be done in solitude; isolated and sequestered. But you don't have to make the journey alone. In allowing those you love to accompany you on the path to discovery and acknowledgement of self, you are both strengthening and securing the bonds that exist between you and others. Do this so that you can learn and grow together as well as individuals.

# FORTY-EIGHT

*'Some of us think holding on makes us strong; but sometimes it is letting go.'*

—*Hermen Hesse*

If the only thing you have in common is the past, then it's time to let go. Realizing and understanding that you have reached a level of growth no longer in tune with another's, is a painful, but necessary part of the journey. Move forward in your path with comfort and peace of mind.

You can look back fondly at the relationship for what it was, but at the same time understand and accept what it ultimately became. Live free of guilt, by releasing yourself from a misplaced obligation to the past.

# FORTY-NINE

*'It is the peculiar quality of a fool, to perceive the faults of others, and to forget his own.'*

—*Marcus Tullius Cicero*

Humans are inherently fallible. Despite all that we think we know; we will never truly be without weakness or fault. That's what makes the pursuit of excellence so important. It's a practice in accountability that keeps us on our toes. Keeps us focused on the journey ahead. Where truth and understanding are our companions, and the potential to lose our way lessens.

To know and understand your fallacies does not mean condoning or accepting them but being aware of them. Recognize when you are about to make a choice that will fall prey to them. Perspective keeps you from succumbing.

# FIFTY

*'Don't judge each day by the harvest you reap, but the seeds that you plant.'*

—*Robert Louis Stevenson*

Some days will be better than others, but don't focus on that. Instead, focus on doing the best you can. Wake up each day and tell yourself 'Today, I'm going to do THE BEST I CAN!' Repeat it throughout the day as often as you need to stay motivated to push through whatever barriers exist. Be they mentally, emotionally or spiritually.

# FIFTY-ONE

*'We are what we repeatedly do. Excellence, then, is not an act, but a habit.'*

—*Aristotle*

Live and exist in the habit of excellence. It becomes habitual and instinctual. Your actions, guided by sincere intent, will you to a purposeful future. Intent means nothing without action and integrity. Be a person of your word and expect no less from others. If you constantly have to question others or they you, it will be impossible to reach the level of understanding needed to be and do your absolute best.

# FIFTY-TWO

*'Every day, I like to wake up and remind myself to be grateful of the simple things.'*

—*Miranda Kerr*

Each day is unique. Today isn't yesterday, and tomorrow won't be today. It is very easy to blame the past as reasons not to push yourself. If you are really committed to making an impact, you must be sincere in your commitment to self. Giving your truest and best effort to manifest the desired results.

# FIFTY-THREE

*'The truth is that every single relationship is very complex and full of contradictions; as you get into a more mature relationship, you realize that the contrasts are part of the fabric of every substantive relationship.'*
—Tony Goldwyn

There is no substitute for substance. Time is precious and limited, therefore should not be wasted with negative thoughts and toxic actions or interactions. Every relationship needs to be symbiotic and reciprocal. Perspective is the gift that keeps on giving. It opens your eyes to the truth of what's working in your favor as well as what isn't. So be savage in your quest for knowledge and growth. Create an environment of purpose and passion all around you.

# FIFTY-FOUR

*'It's your place in the world; it's your life. Go on and do all you can with it, and make it the life you want to live.'*

—*Mae Jemison*

The tiniest spark of passion is all you need to jumpstart your journey. That feeling of anxiety pushing you towards something. That voice that refuses to be quiet any longer; leaving you feeling compelled to act. Look inward to cultivate and nurture that which already exists. It's yours; use it and own it.

# FIFTY-FIVE

*'It is not a person or situation that affects your life; it is the meaning you give to that person or situation, which influences your emotions and actions.'*

—*Shannon L. Alder*

Have the strength to let go. Letting go isn't easy. Negative emotions act as a protective shield between you and the pain you have been avoiding. No one wants to hurt, but by repelling the pain you are slowing the healing process. It takes tremendous strength and courage to abandon the safety of anger, and let pain in. But once you have done so, you can begin to move forward in your journey back to living.

# FIFTY-SIX

*'Worry about your character, not your reputation.'*

—*John Wooden*

There is no shame or weakness in having a loving, giving and open heart. Never let anyone make you feel ashamed because you gave them the benefit of the doubt. Trusting and believing in someone does not make you weak, it makes you true. There will always be those who let us down. That reflects their lack of character; not yours, for wanting to believe in them.

# FIFTY-SEVEN

*'Nothing happens to you; it happens for you.'*

—Joel Osteen

There will be times when you know that the journey ahead will be fraught with pain, but it is necessary to reach the level of clarity you need to grow. It is those times that will require you to fight. To move fearlessly knowing that on the other side of that pain, destiny and truth awaits. Be stronger than you've ever been, so that you can garner the perspective you need to fulfill your purpose.

# FIFTY-EIGHT

*'Well done is better than well said.'*

—*Benjamin Franklin*

Let giving back be, not just an action, but a reflection of how you live and who you are. Don't let humility be overshadowed, or humanity overlooked, when taking the blessings, you've been given to help others navigate their way back to life. Inspire through action. Motivate by example.

# FIFTY-NINE

*'What wisdom can you find that is greater than kindness?'*

—Jean-Jacques Rousseau

Let today be the day you become one with kindness and generosity. Not only with others, but also yourself. Surrender ego and self-importance in exchange for grace and humility. Be generous and gentle with your thoughts, your actions and your words.

# SIXTY

*'The only think you sometimes have control over is perspective.'*

—*Chris Pine.*

Have the courage to free yourself from the past. Be confident in your ability without looking back. Know that you are without a doubt capable of reaching your goals. Past choices and actions should not keep you from having the life you want. Reclaim what is yours. Focus on that which you can control; your present and your future. A life of peace, prosperity and purpose is within reach.

# SIXTY-ONE

*'We can never obtain peace in the outer world until we make peace with ourselves.'*

—Dalai Lama

There are times when it feels like the world is against you, but that couldn't be further from the truth. The consequences of the choices we make, good and bad, reflect our true intent. When your heart and soul are sincere; when you have truly shed ego and move through life with a positive mind and humble heart, will you begin to realize goodness. The universe is on your side. It is rooting for you. It wants you to succeed. Success lies within the process of your progression.

# SIXTY-TWO

*'Energy is the currency of the universe.'*

—*Emily Maroutian*

How others react and respond to us reflects how we perceive and treat ourselves. Our innermost feelings about who we think we are manifest outward and attract like energy back to us. To change outer perceptions, you must change your inner perspective. If you see yourself as confident and strong, so will the world. Love and respect yourself. Give yourself the benefit of the doubt. Open your heart and mind to receive all the blessings and gifts you deserve.

# SIXTY-THREE

*'Angels around us, angels beside us, angels within us.'*

*—Angel Blessing*

I believe that Angels walk among us. They are continuously testing us as human beings. They test our strength. They test our faith, but most importantly they test our humility. Challenging our arrogance to see who will rise above and who will not. They put us in situations that rock our foundation to see how we not only react but respond when given the chance to do something extraordinary.

# SIXTY-FOUR

*'With integrity you have nothing to fear, since you have
nothing to hide.'*

—*Zig Ziglar*

Make doing what's right the rule, not the exception. Strengthen your metaphysical core by being kind, generous and grateful. Have the courage to live empowered by who you are now and will eventually become.

# SIXTY-FIVE

*'We are what we repeatedly do. Excellence, then, is not an act, but a habit.'*

—*Aristotle*

Expect and accept no less than the best; from others or yourself. Be in the habit of excellence, and you will no longer ask yourself if you are doing the right thing. Your heart will guide you to a life filled with power and purpose.

# SIXTY-SIX

*'Be yourself; everyone else is already taken.'*

—*Oscar Wilde*

You and only you set the bar of your achievements. You cannot measure your purpose against the value of another's accomplishments or standards. It's called doing YOUR best. Not his, her or their best. YOU dictate and decide if you have passed the test on your quest to achieve and maintain an elevated standard of purpose and perspective.

# SIXTY-SEVEN

*'There is nothing my mind can conceive, my heart can believe, my eyes can see and my soul can visualize that I cannot do.'*

—Dr. Bien Sufficient

When you feel yourself losing perspective, there are four steps to regaining focus. First, you need to VISUALIZE. Visualize what it is that you want to achieve. Then you must PURSUE. Pursue it with a passion and veracity unparalleled. When you do that you will eventually ATTAIN the perspective needed to understand and appreciate your intent. And lastly, you will REALIZE the benefits and reap the spiritual rewards of reaching your long-desired goals.

# SIXTY-EIGHT

*'Excellence is never an accident.'*

*—Aristotle*

If cleanliness is next to Godliness, then excellence is next to divinity. Anything and everything you do should be done with the intention of doing your best. Not jst in word, but in actions. If you pursue excellence and aim to have perspective in all areas of your life, you won't worry about things working out. You will have trained yourself to accept nothing but the best. If for any reason you begin to get distracted, your inner self will do what is necessary to get you back on track.

When you hold yourself accountable, a place of divinity and peace will be reached. That calming place of clarity where everything you want and need is laid out before you.

# SIXTY-NINE

*'No more martyring myself.'*

*—Sharon E. Rainey*

There is nothing wrong with loving, supporting and encouraging others. However, it should not be done to the detriment of your own mental, emotional and spiritual well-being. Help others by being an example, not a crutch. Refuse to allow them to bankrupt your spirituality or empty your emotional vault.

# SEVENTY

*'Be kinder to yourself. And then let your kindness flood the world.'*

—*Pema Chodron*

We spend a lifetime serving others. Our own wants and needs getting lost in the shuffle; overshadowed, overlooked and ignored. Give yourself the love, attention affection and understanding that has been denied in priority of others.

# SEVENTY-ONE

*'The simple things can be really powerful.'*

—Jon Taffer

Take the time to enjoy the simple things. Let your spirit and your soul roam free. Remember how special you are and reflect on a time before dreams were replaced with duty. Before dreams were replaced with duty, and passions gave way to obligations. You have a place in this world, so before you settle for a life unrecognizable to your former self; remember, retake and reclaim your destiny.

# SEVENTY-TWO

*'Trust instinct to the end, even though you can give no reason.'*

—*Ralph Waldo Emerson*

If you feel you are being pulled towards or away from something, that is instinct. And it is real. It's there to guide you in your journey and keep you on course. There to keep you from being distracted by what you want, instead of accepting what you need. It is a warning that your life's purpose is at stake. The growth and understanding you have worked so hard to achieve is at in danger of being eroded.

# SEVENTY-THREE

*'You're always with yourself, so you might as well enjoy the company.'*

—*Diane Von Furstenberg*

To experience true and unconditional love, you must start by loving yourself. Acknowledge, accept and respect who you are. Find comfort and solace in the arms of self-love and you will attract the love you need.

# SEVENTY-FOUR

*'We must reach out for our full potential. The potential lies in our inner strength.'*

—Laila Gifty Akita

Approach each day with positivity, perspective and energy. There is no better time to have all that you desire than now. There is no better time to live than today. The opportunities to achieve excellence are everywhere. So, be purposeful in your intention.

# SEVENTY-FIVE

*'An attitude of gratitude brings great things.'*

—Yogi Bhajan

No matter how overwhelmed you may be at the time, there is no such thing as too far, too long, too high or too hard. Take things one day, one task and one goal at a time. This will ensure success at every level of your existence. Life is precious, and time a blessing. Use it to take advantage, but not for granted, all the resources at your disposal to be better every day. When you live a truly grateful life, acknowledge and appreciate your blessings, you will live in abundance and prosperity.

# SEVENTY-SIX

*'I was always looking outside myself for strength and confidence, but it comes from within. It is there all the time.'*

—*Anna Freud*

When you are committed to adversity and the struggles you are going through, the sheer thought of making it through seems as impossible as it does improbable. The only way to ensure your lack of survival is to give up. But if you tap into the strength and passion inside; harness and bring it to the surface, you will have the power you need to not only endure but move past what is holding you back.

# SEVENTY-SEVEN

*'Humans see what they want to see.'*

—*Rick Riordan*

Do not let your heart, your spirit or your future be contingent on that of another. Be confident and strong in your resolve. Commit to loving, respecting, embracing and most importantly forgiving yourself. Another person's perception should never cloud your own. Your strength lies in the clarity and perspective you have achieved.

# SEVENTY-EIGHT

*'Neither age nor experience matters when it comes to being personally accountable for any and all outcomes.'*

—*Kory Livingstone*

Accountability is one of the first steps towards perspective and resulting freedom. Bur first you must admit and accept your role in the separation of destiny and truth; acknowledgement and understanding.

When you accept, acknowledge and appreciate that the world isn't all about you, you will have freed yourself of the responsibility of being constantly wronged. The burden of always taking things personally, and yourself too seriously, will have been lifted. You can the resume your journey to mental, emotional and spiritual freedom.

# SEVENTY-NINE

*'The better you become, the less time it takes you to achieve your goals.'*

—*Brian Tracy*

We invest so much of our time, our energies and our emotions in others that we forget the most important investment of all; in ourselves. True wealth and power begin within. This cannot be done if others can empty your spiritual resources and keep you from a place of peace and clarity. Invest in your mental health, emotional well-being and spiritual growth so that you will have the energy you need to share the wealth and knowledge with others.

# EIGHTY

*'Never does a man portray his character more vividly than when proclaiming the character of another.'*

—*Winston Churchill*

Some traits can't be learned or taught. You're either born with them or you're not. But I believe that most people are. Character, empathy, integrity and kindness are inherent within you. Nurture them, grow them and hold yourself accountable to them. Have high expectations, not just of others, but of yourself. Be sincere in your actions and maintain perspective in your reactions.

# EIGHTY-ONE

*'Do you want to be safe and good, or do you want to take a chance and be great?'*

—Jimmy Johnson

Have the courage to free yourself from the past. Be confident in your ability to live in the present without looking back. Don't be afraid to take chances. Reject the safe and comfortable and explore the irrational and unpredictable. Those risks that on the outside seem insane, but that you know hold the key to your future. You are more than capable of unlocking your potential and reaching your goals.

# EIGHTY-TWO

*'Never give up and don't ask why, because every situation does not need an answer.'*

—Eric Davis

Don't waste valuable energy asking why. At the end of the day, it doesn't really matter. What does matter is what you are going to do about it. Stop wasting time and energy on the wrong things. The problem instead of the solution. We do the same thing when it comes to our past choices. Using them to justify our present actions by wallowing in self-pity. Focusing on what you did previously to get where you are now, means nothing compared to what you're going to do to move forward. Forgive your past, accept your present and believe in your future.

# EIGHTY-THREE

*'We should not, therefore, be afraid of testing others—or of being tested ourselves.'*

*—Sandra Byrd*

Life is full of tests. Opportunities to show who we are and what we are made of. When most think of being tested, the first thing that comes to mind is faith. There is another test frequently overlooked tests of grace. Graciousness is a way of living, being. There are times we get the chance to be gracious, and how we proceed affects our standing in the universe. It will know, and decide, who is worthy of its blessings. Choose wisely.

# EIGHTY-FOUR

*'Kindness connects to who you are, while niceness connects to
how you want to be seen.'*

—David Levithan

There is a difference between being nice and being kind. Nice is just that...nice.
Doing just enough for others to give the impression, or rather illusion, that it is
being done out of kindness. But these nice gestures last as long as it doesn't
interfere with their agenda or intrude on their own wants and needs. Being nice is a
superficial trait, skin deep. It is attention seeking and driven by ego. But being kind,
is soul deep. A quiet thoughtfulness that exists in the gestures put forth. In kindness,
there is commitment and integrity and commitment to integrity. One driven by the
act itself and not the resulting praise, adoration or adulation. True kindness is not in
need of validation.

# EIGHTY-FIVE

*'Even where there is talent, culture, knowledge, if there is not earnestness, it does not go to the root of things.'*

—James Freeman Clarke

Intention is everything, so be sincere in your actions and words. Be willing to strip yourself naked and bare the rawest part of your soul. If you seek perspective with sincerity of heart and spirit, you will reach levels that you never dreamed possible.

# EIGHTY-SIX

*'Don't do nothing because you can't do everything. Do something. Anything.'*

—*Colleen Patrick-Goudreau*

When deciding to do something, the only reason you need is that you can. It doesn't matter what it is. Just do something. Do it because you have the ability. Therein lies the power; your power. Take a walk. Go for a swim. Call a friend. Make an apology, accept an apology. Make amends or make a change. Do it because you can.

# EIGHTY-SEVEN

*'The only thing standing between you and your goal is the bullshit story you keep telling yourself as to why you can't achieve it.'*

—*Jordan Belfort*

If you are busy making moves, you won't have the time or energy to make excuses. You won't even want to. You will not care to turn around, because looking back will no longer be an option. Keep your goals in front of you and pursue with intent. Not unlike a cross-country drive, when it comes to life, one thing is abundantly clear; if you keep moving forward, you will eventually get there.

# EIGHTY-EIGHT

*'The man who complains about the way the ball bounces, is likely to be the one who dropped it.'*

—*Lou Holtz*

Perspective is about so much more than the way one views things. It carries a power that can only be achieved when you gain clarity through accountability and responsibility. That power allows you to approach every situation, encounter and relationship enlightened and empowered.

Accepting responsibility means you are not a victim, but in total control of your life and its direction. The more perspective you gain, the clearer your path will become; the more opportunities will come your way. When this happens, open yourself to making bigger and bolder choices. More aggressive, assertive and confident ones. Be relentless in your pursuit, purposeful in your thoughts and deliberate in your actions.

# EIGHTY-NINE

*'Choices are the hinges of destiny.'*

—*Edwin Markham*

It doesn't take a new year to begin anew. Every moment you have a chance to change your thinking and your actions. It isn't about winning, but the opportunity to win. Give yourself the chance to succeed by making better choices. Financial, emotional, romantic. Spiritual, physical and mental. Little things make big differences. Not only in our lives, but in the lives of those we love.

# NINETY

*'Risk is the sort of word that is easy to discuss upfront, but tough to handle when it comes time to pay the piper.'*

—*Nathan Myhrvold*

We all have choices to make. There will come a time when you have to ask yourself: Can I? Will I? Is it possible to abandon the security and stability of tradition for the unstable, insecure and unpredictable life of one on the edge of greatness? You have one life to live, so stop second guessing yourself.

# NINETY-ONE

*'Don't stay with me because you feel bad for me. I don't need your pity. Stay with me because you want to.'*

—*thatonerule #703*

Don't confuse gratitude with love. Loving the things someone does for you, rather than loving who they are. As individuals we make our own decisions, our own choices. You are not obligated to someone because of what they themselves choose to do for you. Guilt, obligation and duty are three reasons NOT to be with someone. Instead, you should be driven by love, happiness and passion.

# NINETY-TWO

*'The most special relationships, in my experience, are based on a combination of trust and mutual respect.'*

—*Charles Kennedy*

There is no greater, more rewarding, feeling than mutual love and respect between you and those you care about. Their wins are your wins, and their losses you feel in your own heart of where your relationship lies- good, bad or in-between, take the time to say 'Thank you. Congratulations. I miss you. I'm sorry.' Let humility take over and place your heart on the sleeve of the universe.

# NINETY-THREE

*'I do not think much of a man who is not wiser today than he was yesterday.'*

—*Abraham Lincoln*

How you start your journey to truth and perspective in no way dictates how you finish it. You must be flexible. Be open minded and committed because the road is not straight and winding.

The day will go on with or without you. Don't waste it in a negative space. Spend it making opportunities instead of excuses. Don't let stubbornness cloud your clarity and keep you in a state of being void of understanding. There are always things we don't want to do, but they are necessary on the path to progression.

# NINETY-FOUR

*'You may not control all the events that happen to you, but you can decide not to be reduced by them.'*

—*Maya Angelou*

Be grateful. Choose happiness and living. Life and love. Choose forgiveness, peace and positivity. You can be simultaneously humble and proud. Be happy with who you are, yet never stop striving to be the best you possible.

# NINETY-FIVE

*'Putting a voice to your soul helps you to let go of the negative energy of fear and regret.'*

—*Shannon L. Adler*

You will know when energies, focus and attentions have shifted. You will have reached a point of accountability and inevitability within yourself, where every decision, every action and every choice made has fate filled duties and pre-destined consequences and outcomes. There will be no more time for the chaos of conflict, the anxiety of indecision or the frivolity of drama. There will be no more time for regrets, guilt or looking back. No, instead only forward thinking and forward actions.

# NINETY-SIX

*'The sooner we heal our traumas, the sooner we liberate ourselves from the people who hurt us.'*

—*Vironika Tugaleva*

Letting go may be painful in the immediate sense, but that is simply the pain of the past escaping and releasing you. Unlocking your present and unchaining your future. Leaving you free to achieve everything that destiny has planned for you. Instead of crawling from the wreckage of devastation and humiliation, walk tall and proud with your dignity intact. Triumphant full of strength and passion. With the understanding and acceptance that you did the right thing.

# NINETY-SEVEN

*'If you're going to trust one person, let it be yourself.'*

—Robert Tew

Trust yourself. That feeling in your gut is the universe's way of telling you that you are right. So pay attention. We all go through the motions. Wondering where we fit, where we're going. If we're making the right choices. It's not the question, but the answer that matters. Stop ignoring your purpose and denying your destiny. Stop putting off the inevitable to avoid an outcome you know is coming anyway.

# NINETY-EIGHT

*'I am only going to say what I want to put into the universe.'*
*—Positivity Note*

Energy is as energy does, so put out positive vibes whenever you can. Don't just read it and repeat it but live it. Life really can be that good. Not because it is perfect, but because it's the perspective you choose. Everyone's journey, purpose, path and truth are uniquely their own. Don't disparage, chastise or judge. The universe speaks to you where you are. Encourage, inspire and understand others.

# NINETY-NINE

*'When we lose one blessing, another is often most unexpectedly given in its place.'*

—C.S. Lewis

Blessings and lessons exist in the things that don't happen, as much as in the things that do. This is important to know and understand because it opens the mind to the possibilities that exist to fill the space in your life, that is now available for something fresh. Something new.

# ONE HUNDRED

*'Never underestimate the power of dreams and the influence of the human spirit. We are all the same in this notion: The potential for greatness lives within each of us.*

—*Wilma Rudolph*

It is just as rewarding to make another's day, as it is to have someone make yours. Be good to yourself by being good to someone else. It doesn't have to be some grandiose or dramatic gesture but be mindful. Don't underestimate the value your presence adds to another person's life, and the unknowing positive impact you can make. Not just in their day, but their life.

There are many wonderful things just waiting on the horizon, and it only requires that you participate. Take today and make it yours.

Made in the USA
San Bernardino,
CA

58536004R00068